DISCARD

Jefferson School
West Allis, WI

THE SUN

Design	David West Children's Book Design
Designer	Keith Newell
Editor	Denny Robson
Picture Researcher	Emma Krikler
Illustrator	Guy Smith, Mainline Design

© Aladdin Books 1991

First published in
the United States in 1991 by
Gloucester Press
387 Park Avenue South
New York NY 10016

Library of Congress Cataloging-in-Publication Data

Robson, Denny.
    The sun / by Denny Robson.
       p.   cm. -- (Let's look up)
    Includes index.
    Summary: Examines the sun, discussing heat, light, plants and sunlight, fossil fuels, and energy.
    ISBN 0-531-17336-4
    1. Sun--Juvenile literature. 2. Solar radiation--Juvenile literature. 3. Solar energy--Juvenile literature. (1. Sun.)
I.Title.
QB521.5.R63   1991
523.7--dc20   91-10316   CIP
                                           AC

Printed in Belgium

All rights reserved

LET'S LOOK UP

THE SUN

DENNY ROBSON

GLOUCESTER PRESS
New York : London : Toronto : Sydney

CONTENTS

The birth of the Sun	6
The Sun's family	8
Inside the Sun	10
The stormy Sun	12
Sunlight	14
The Sun's heat	16
Eclipse of the Sun	18
One among millions	20
The end of the Sun	22
Looking at the Sun	24
Sun facts	26
Star facts	28
Solar power facts	30
Glossary and index	32

WARNING! It is *always* dangerous to look directly at the Sun. Turn to page 24 to find out how you can study the Sun safely.

About this book
You can decide for yourself how to read this book. You can simply read it straight through. Or you can follow the arrows to find out more about a subject before you go on. The choice is yours!

Follow the arrows if you want to know more....

INTRODUCTION

The Sun is the most important thing in the sky for us. There could be no life on Earth without its heat and light. The Sun is a star, a swirling mass of hot gases spinning around in space. It is just like the other stars you see in the sky at night. They are suns that are far, far away. We see our Sun during the day simply because it is so much closer to us.

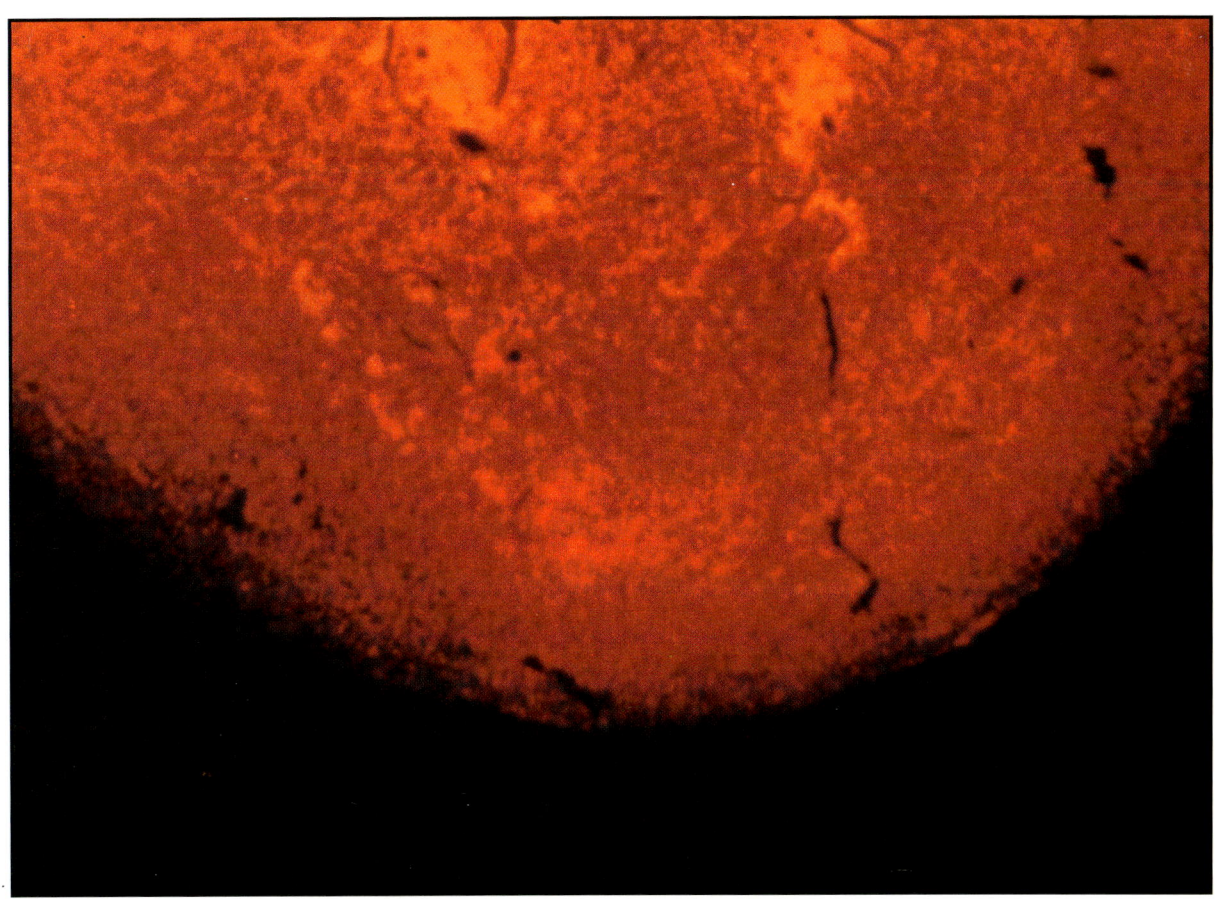

The Sun is a ball of hot gas, a million times bigger than Earth.

△ Our Sun was born from a huge cloud of dust and gas floating in space.

THE BIRTH OF THE SUN

Where did the Sun come from? About 5 billion years ago, there was no Sun, or Earth. Our part of space was filled with a huge cloud of dust and gas. Slowly, gravity pulled this cloud together. It began to shrink and spin faster. The middle of the cloud became thick and hot and finally turned into a giant ball of glowing gas. A new star, our Sun, was born.

Do all stars begin this way?

All stars begin the same way. They are formed in clouds of dust and gas called nebulae.

This is the Orion Nebula, a mass of gas and dust in which stars are born.

If you want to know more about other stars, turn to Star facts → PAGE 28

THE SUN'S FAMILY

As the Sun was being born, planets began to form from the leftover gas and dust which circled the Sun. The planets still travel around the Sun, in oval paths called orbits. In order from the Sun, the planets are Mercury, Venus, Earth, Mars, Jupiter, Saturn, Uranus, Neptune, and Pluto. The Sun and its family of planets together are called the Solar System.

The planets depend on the Sun for their heat and light. Those furthest from the Sun are cold and dark.

Left, frozen Neptune. Above, fiery Venus.

If you want to know more about Earth's orbit around the Sun, turn to Sun facts → PAGE 26

Why do the planets circle the Sun?

The Sun is at the center of the Solar System. The pulling force of its gravity keeps each planet circling around it.

INSIDE THE SUN

The surface of the Sun is called the photosphere. It gives off most of the light we get from the Sun. The energy that keeps the Sun shining is made at its center, or core. Here, the pressure is so great that tiny parts of gas are squeezed together in a process called nuclear fusion. When this happens, heat and light are given off in a huge burst of energy.

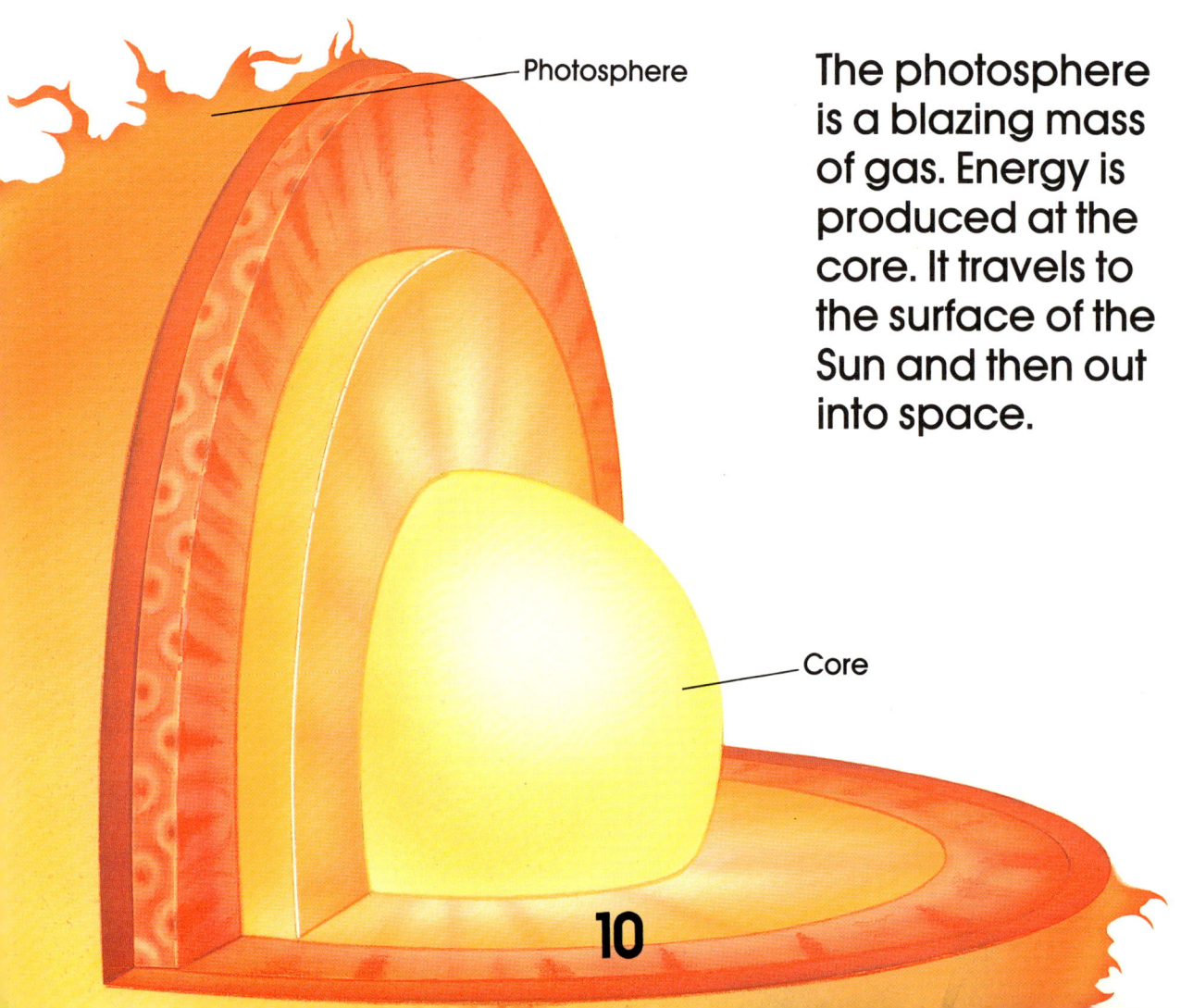

Photosphere

The photosphere is a blazing mass of gas. Energy is produced at the core. It travels to the surface of the Sun and then out into space.

Core

How hot is the Sun?

The Sun is thousands of times hotter than a bonfire. If a spacecraft got too near to the Sun, it would melt!

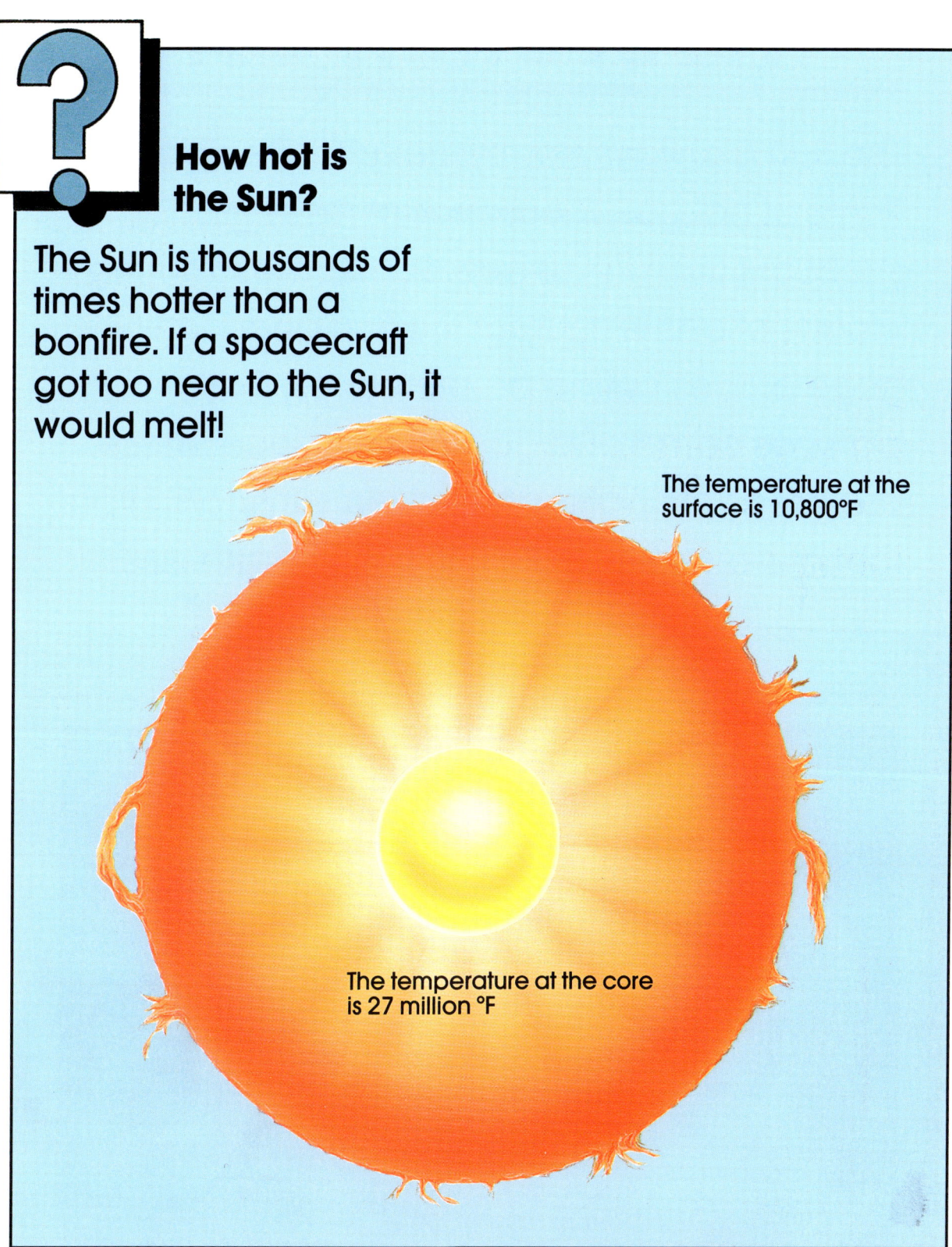

The temperature at the surface is 10,800°F

The temperature at the core is 27 million °F

If you want to know how hot other stars are, turn to Star facts — PAGE 28

THE STORMY SUN

The Sun is always stormy, never calm. Giant flares of hot gas, thousands of miles high, shoot out from its surface. Sometimes flaming clouds of gas leap from the Sun and form huge arches called prominences. Dark patches come and go on the surface. These are areas of cooler gas, called sunspots. Even the smallest "spot" is as big as the Earth!

▽ This is a photograph of the Sun taken by a solar telescope.

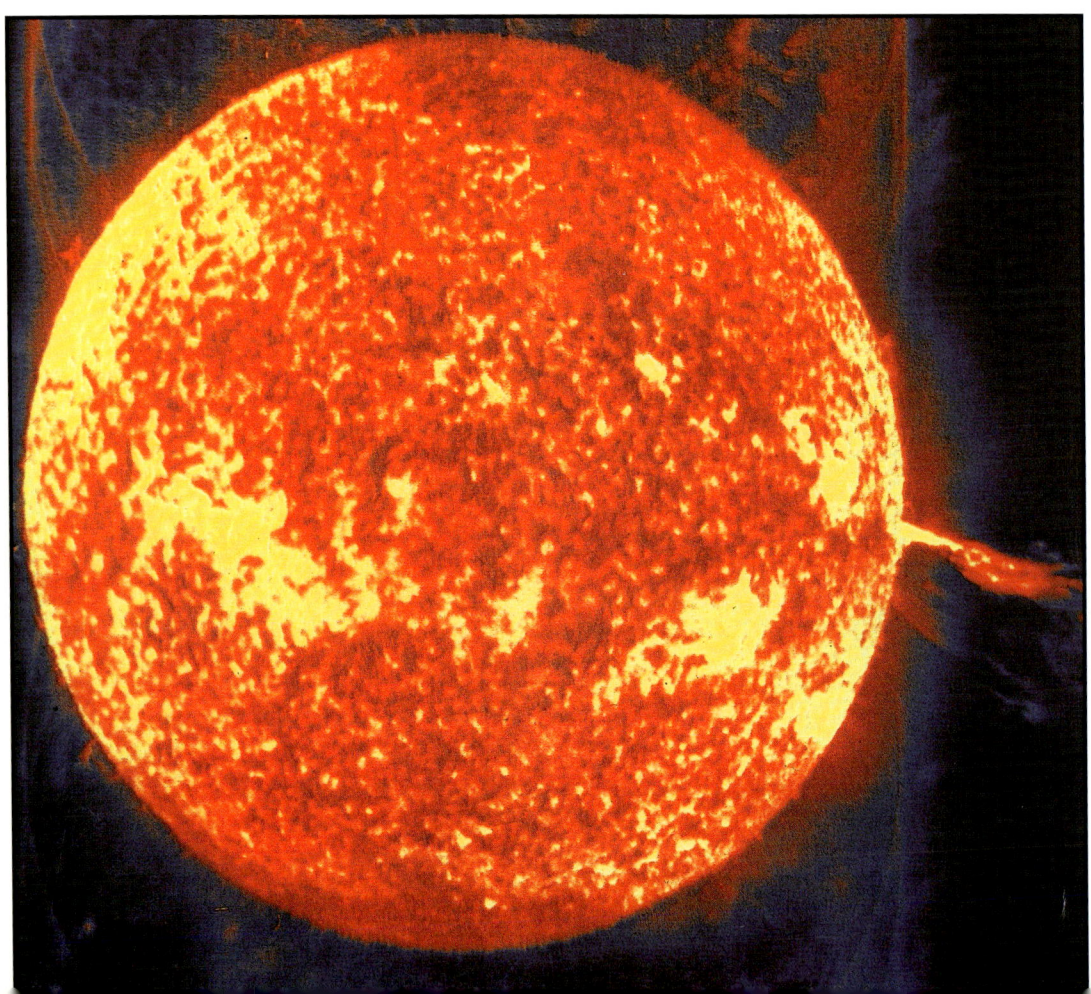

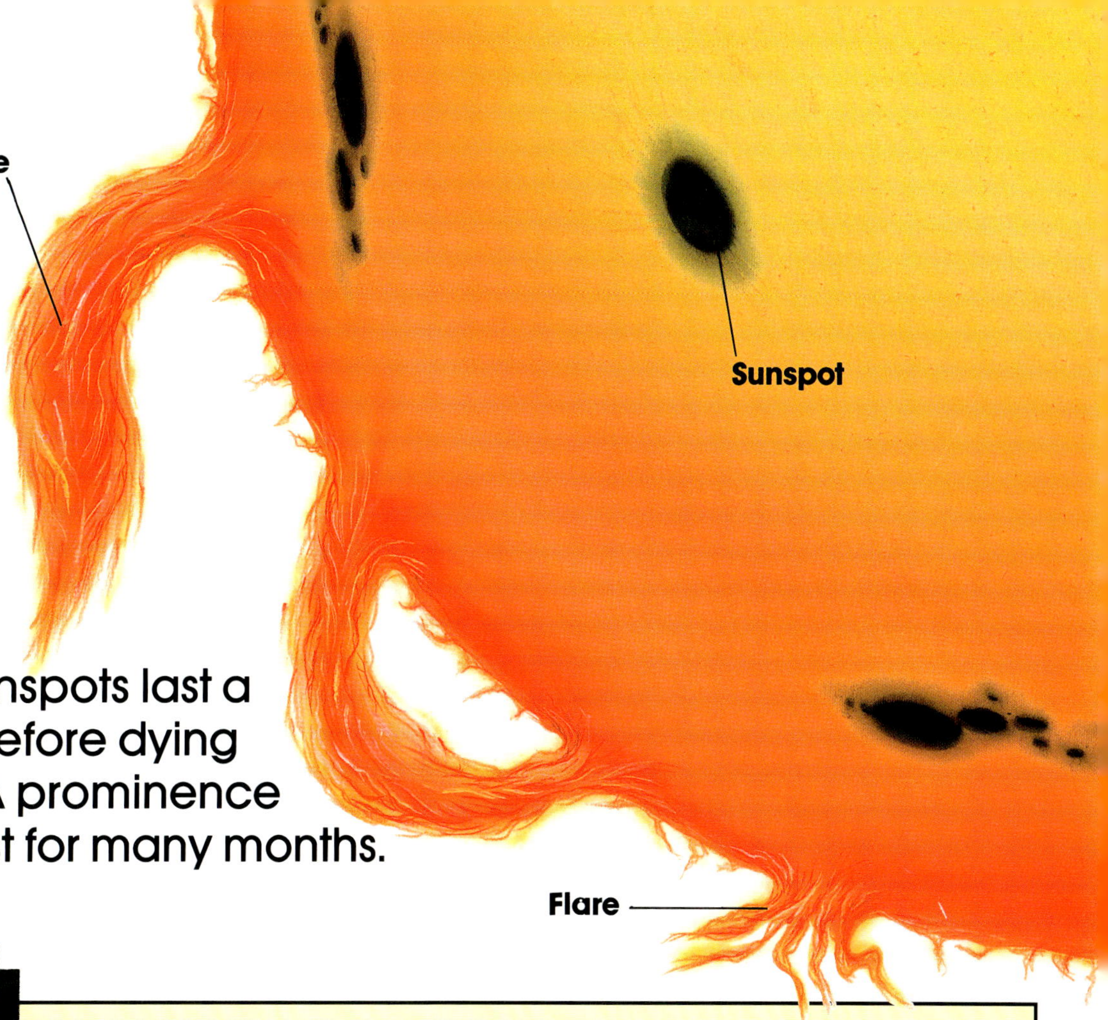

Prominence

Sunspot

Flare

Most sunspots last a week before dying away. A prominence may last for many months.

How do we know about the Sun's stormy surface?

This is a solar telescope. Scientists use it to photograph the storms and dark spots on the Sun's surface.

If you want to know how *you* can safely study the Sun, turn to Looking at the Sun

PAGE 24

SUNLIGHT

All living things need sunlight. Green plants need sunlight to grow. Animals feed on the plants, and people feed on the plants and animals. The Sun also gives us light to see by. On Earth sunlight looks white. But in fact, it is made of many different colors. You can see these colors in a rainbow, when raindrops break up sunlight into its different colors.

Why does the Sun rise and set?

The Sun seems to move across the sky during the day and then disappears at night. But really it is Earth turning.

Find out more about day and night in Sun facts　　　**PAGE 26**

14

As it passes through a prism, sunlight is spread out into its band of colors – red, orange, yellow, green, blue, indigo, and violet.

THE SUN'S HEAT

The Sun warms the Earth. Without its heat, our planet would be a cold, dead place. Its warmth helps food to grow. It also controls the weather. Storms, winds, clouds, and rain are caused by the Sun's heat.

We also use the Sun's energy to make electricity, both on Earth and in space. As other fuels run out, it will become more and more important to use solar power.

We are learning how to use solar power in place of old ways of producing electricity.

How can we use solar power in our homes?

Houses in sunny countries can have solar panels. They collect the Sun's heat and use it to heat water.

Find out more about using the Sun's power in Solar power facts → PAGE 30

ECLIPSE OF THE SUN

Just as Earth travels around the Sun, the Moon travels around Earth. Sometimes, the Moon comes between the Earth and Sun. Then it blocks out the Sun's light and the Moon casts its shadow upon Earth. This is called an eclipse. When the Moon completely covers the Sun, we call it a total eclipse. When only part of it covers the Sun, it is a partial eclipse.

During an eclipse, the Moon passes between Earth and the Sun. The Moon's shadow then falls on part of the Earth.

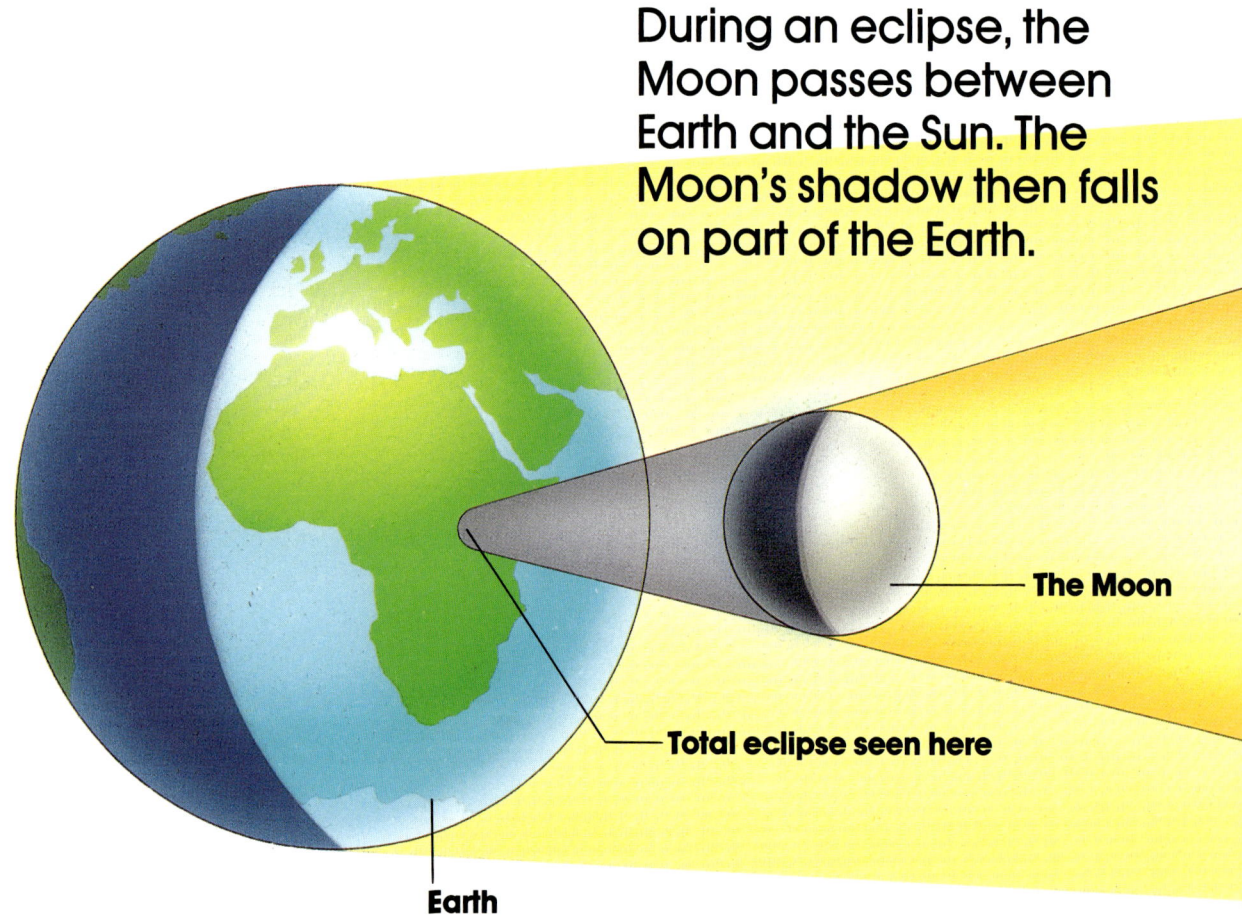

What do you see during an eclipse?

This is a photograph of a total eclipse of the Sun. You can see a circle of glowing gas around the Sun. This is the corona.

If you want to know how to look at the Sun *safely*, turn to Looking at the Sun ➔ PAGE 24

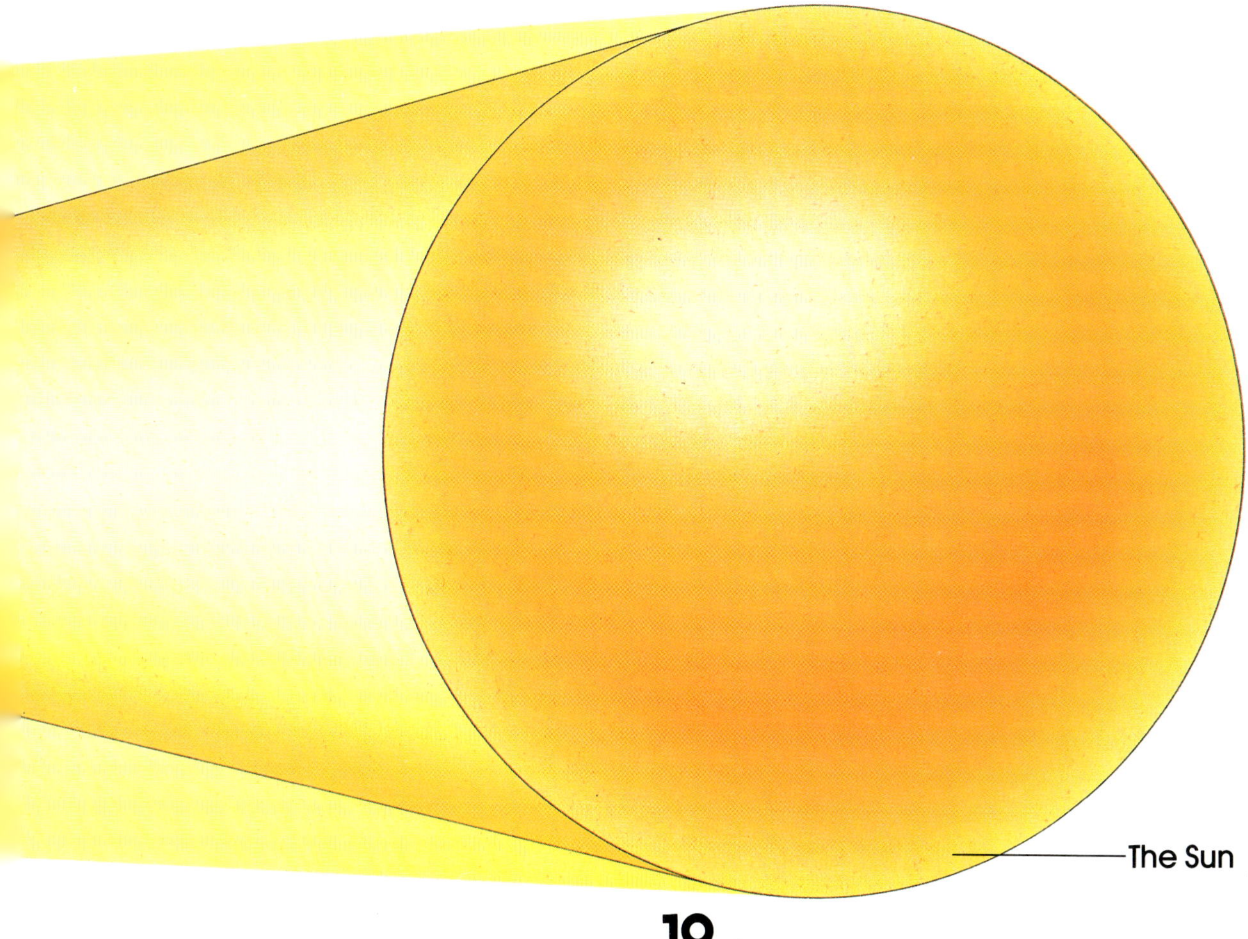

The Sun

19

ONE AMONG MILLIONS

Our Sun is just one of a billion stars in a group of stars called a galaxy. And there are millions of other galaxies in the Universe. The billions of stars that exist in space come in a wide range of sizes and colors and brightnesses. There are even invisible stars called black holes. Compared to all these other suns, our Sun is just a very ordinary star.

△ Our Sun belongs to this galaxy. It is called the Milky Way.

What are black holes?

A very large star explodes at the end of its life. It may shrink into itself and form a black hole. The pull of gravity of a black hole is so strong that even its own light cannot escape! Black holes suck in anything that passes close to them.

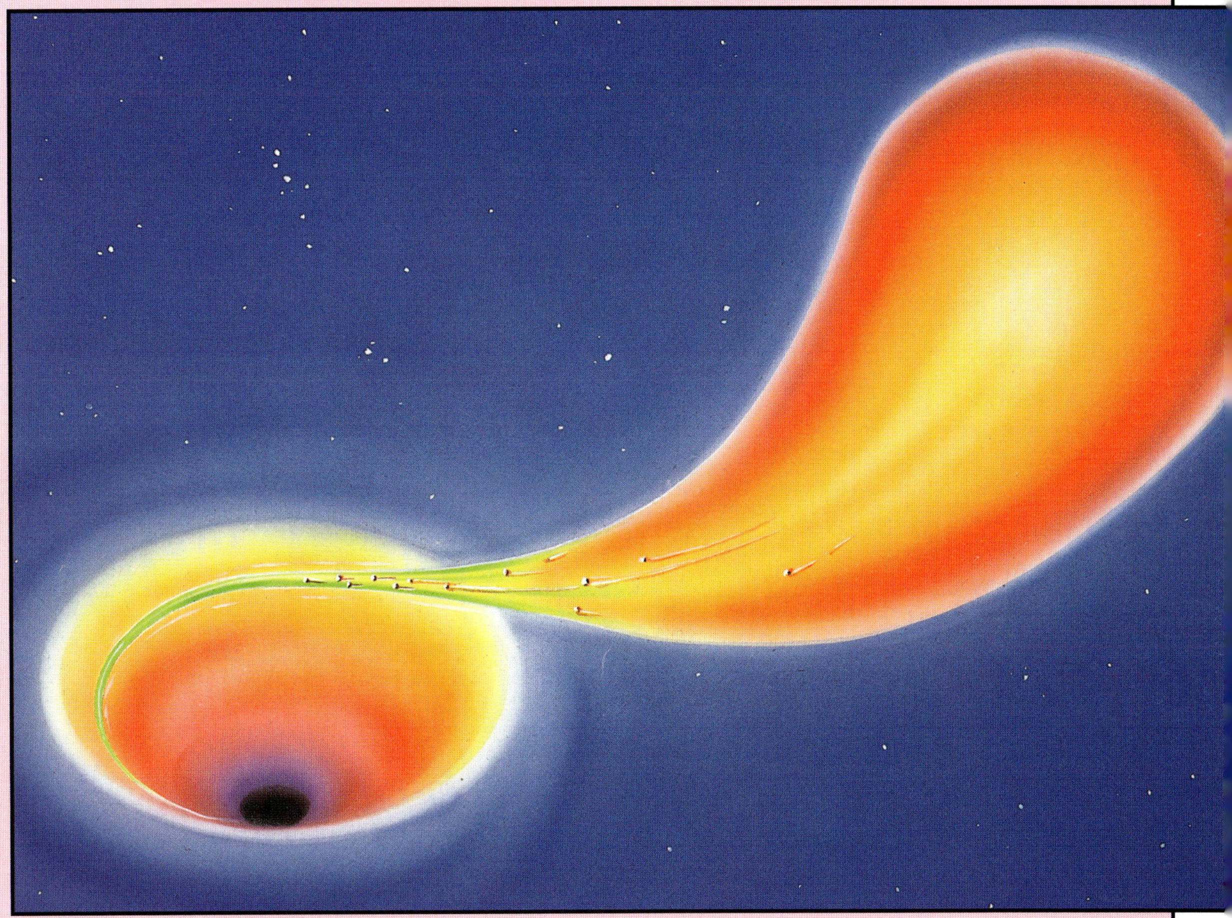

△ A black hole sucks in gas from a nearby star.

Find out more about black holes in Star facts — PAGE 28

THE END OF THE SUN

The Sun is not an old star. It has been shining for 4.6 billion years and it will continue to shine for billions of years to come. But stars do not live forever and one day the Sun will die. It will slowly swell to become a red giant star and then cool down and fade away. Long before this happens, people will begin to look for new stars and new places to live.

How do other stars die?

Different stars end their days in different ways. A star much bigger than our Sun dies in a huge explosion called a supernova.

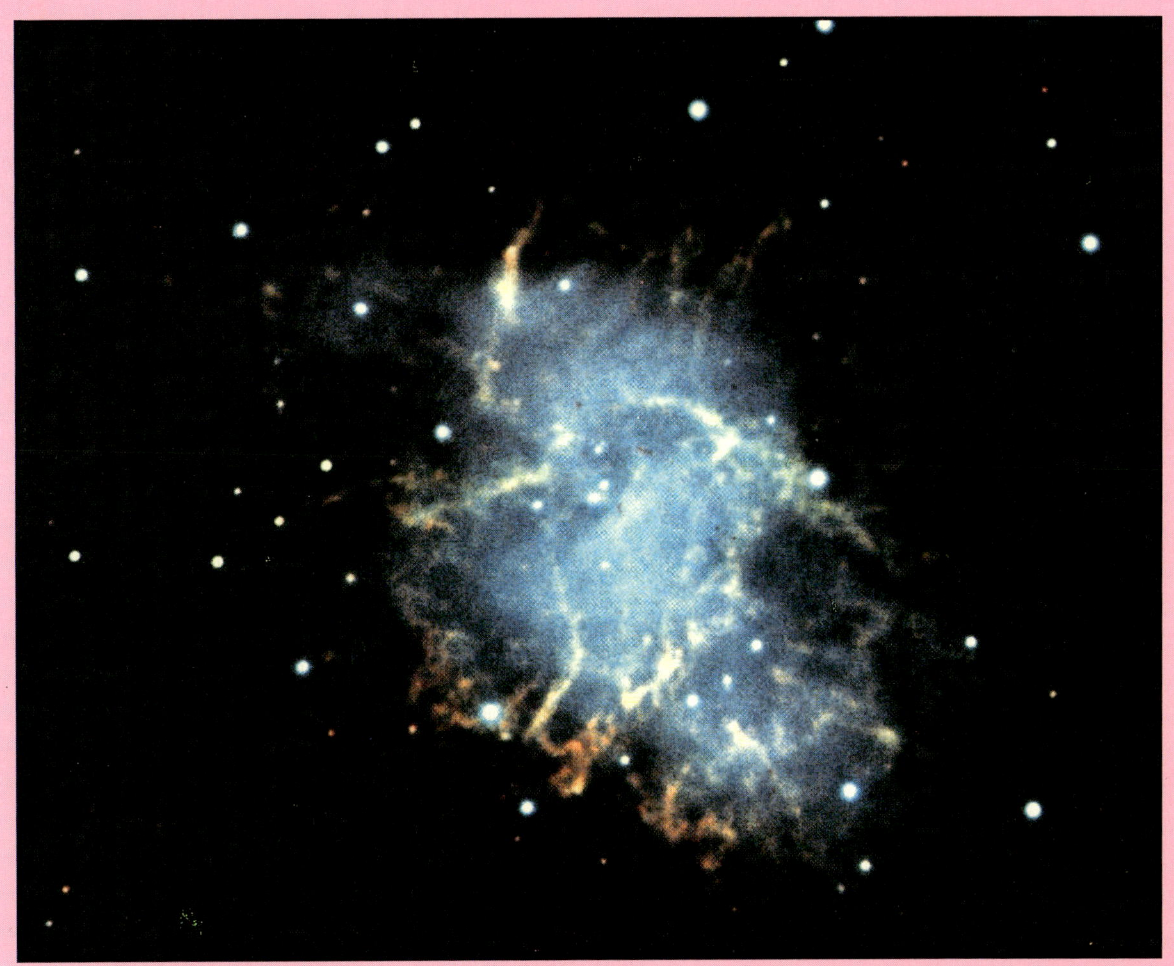

△ This is the Crab Nebula. It is the remains of a star that exploded long ago.

Find out more about star deaths in Star facts PAGE 28

LOOKING AT THE SUN

You must be careful when you look toward the Sun. NEVER look at the Sun through binoculars or a telescope. This could make you blind. Even staring at the Sun is dangerous. In this project you can find out how to observe the Sun safely. You look at an image of the Sun on a piece of cardboard and NOT at the Sun itself. You might be able to see sunspots. See if they change from day to day.

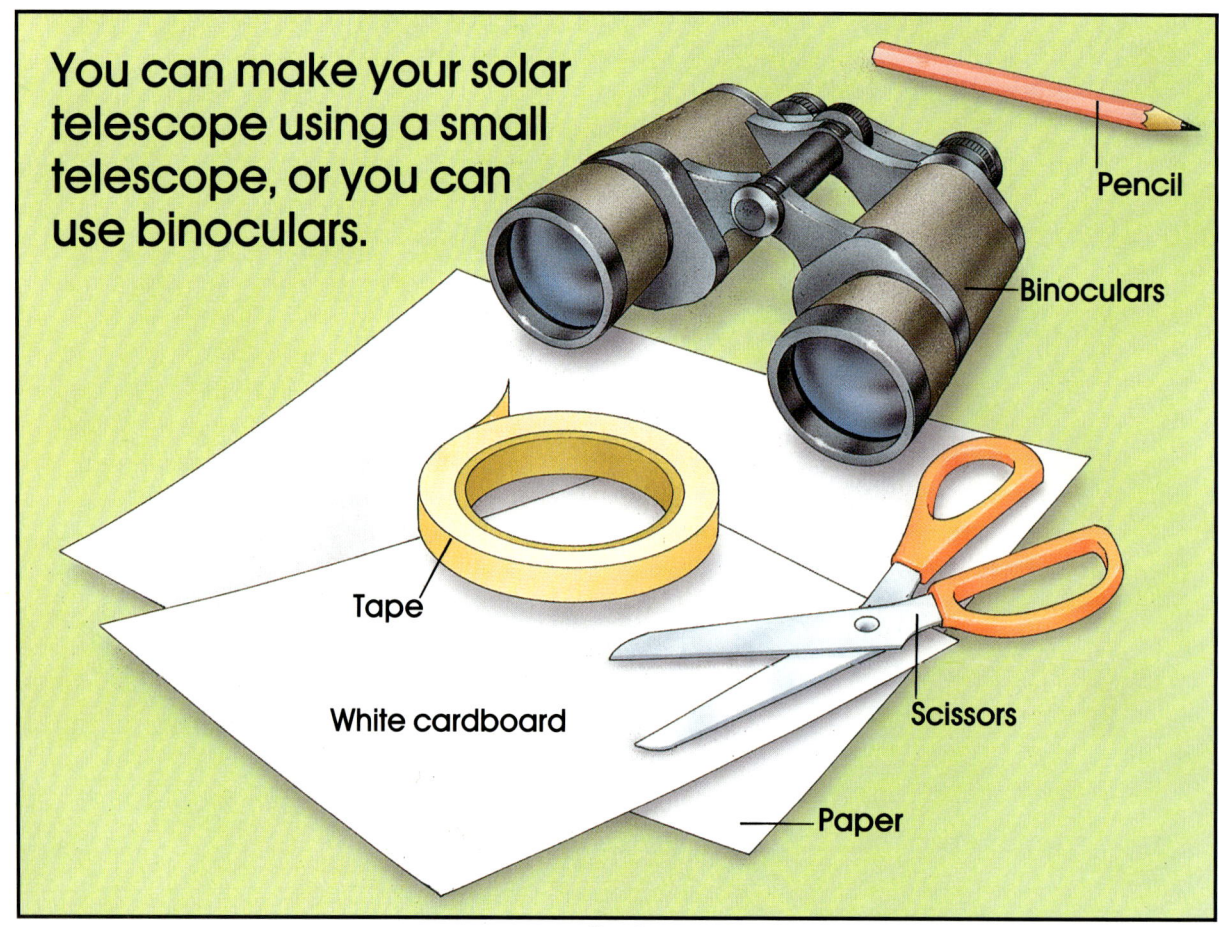

You can make your solar telescope using a small telescope, or you can use binoculars.

Pencil

Binoculars

Tape

White cardboard

Scissors

Paper

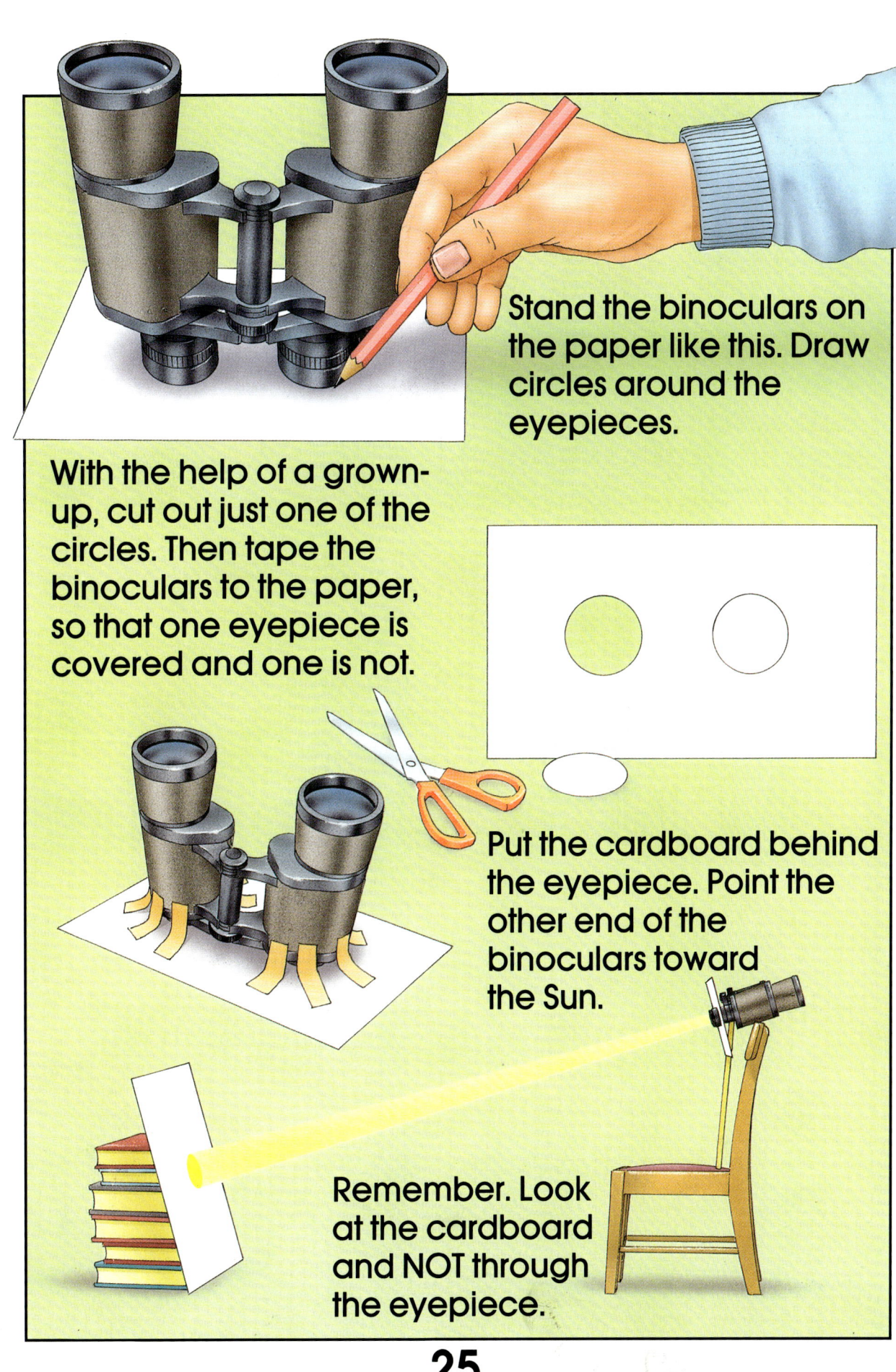

SUN FACTS

Earth takes a year to orbit the Sun. During the year, each place on Earth gets different amounts of sunshine. Here you can see the Earth at different times of the year.

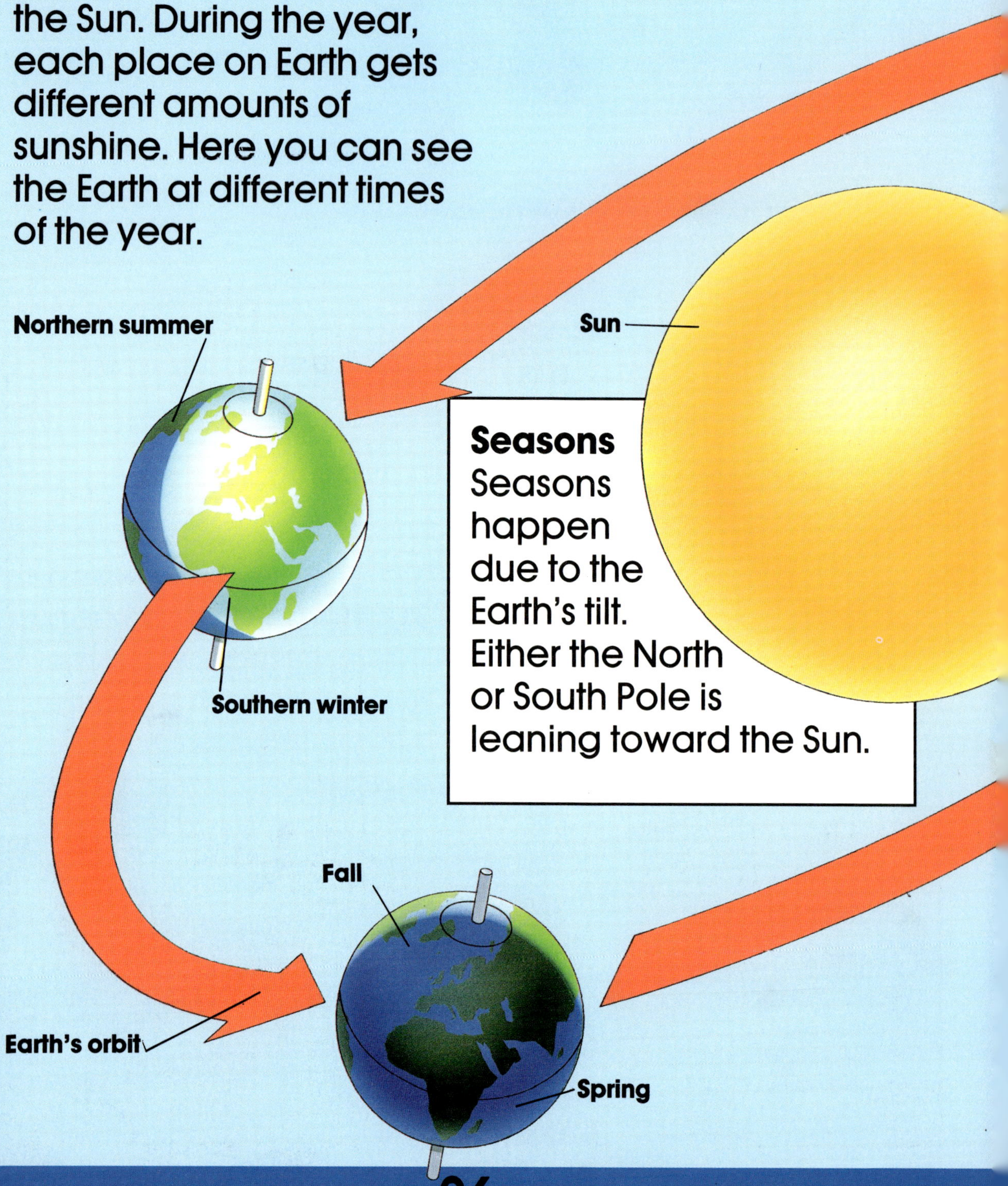

Northern summer

Sun

Southern winter

Seasons
Seasons happen due to the Earth's tilt. Either the North or South Pole is leaning toward the Sun.

Fall

Earth's orbit

Spring

26

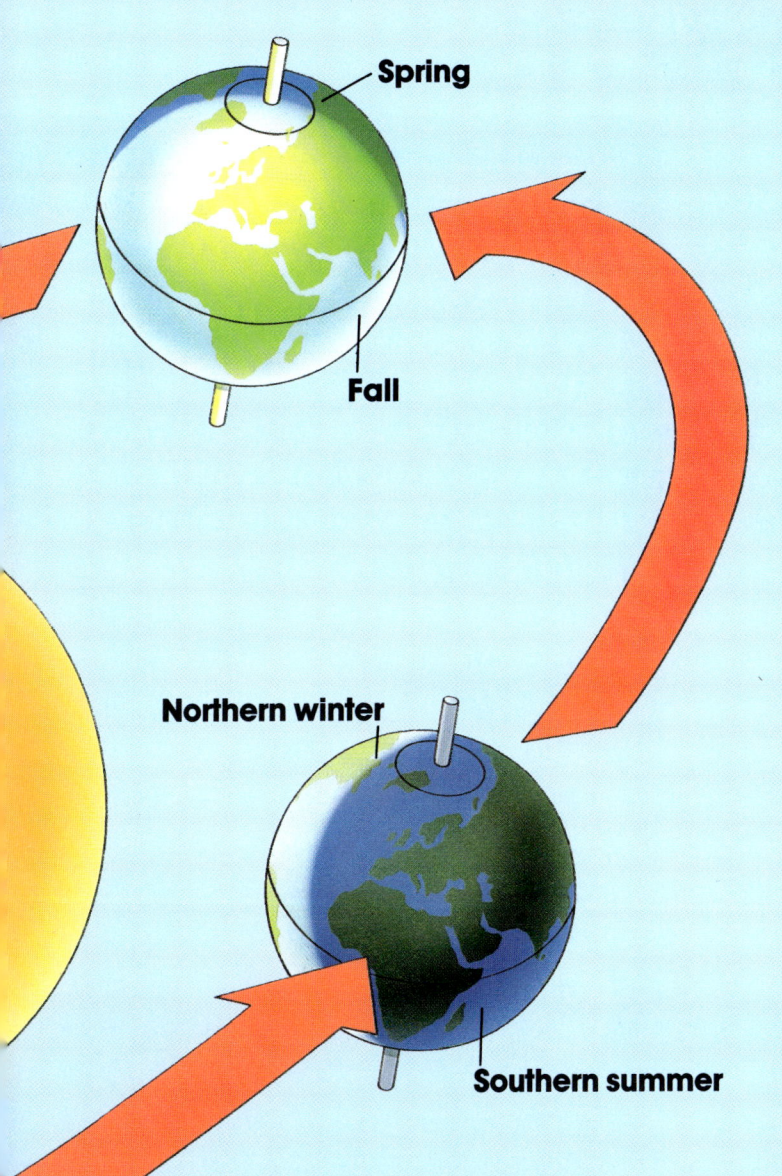

Day and night
The Earth turns around once in 24 hours. It is daytime when our part of the Earth faces the Sun. It is night when that part of the Earth turns away from the Sun.

How far away are the stars? The Sun is 93 million mi away. Look how long it takes light to reach Earth from the next star!

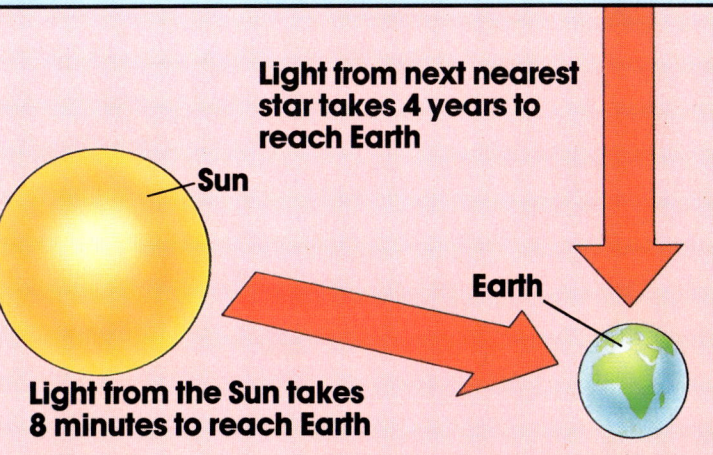

Light from next nearest star takes 4 years to reach Earth

Light from the Sun takes 8 minutes to reach Earth

STAR FACTS

Our Sun is 100 times wider than Earth, but it is not a big star. Very large stars, called supergiants, may be 300 times bigger than our Sun! Stars much smaller than the Sun are called dwarfs.

— Dwarf star

Giant star   Our Sun

Star deaths
1 In the end, stars like our Sun become Red Giants.
2 A much bigger star will explode in a supernova.
3 A very massive star may collapse and become a black hole.

Stars also come in different colors. The color of a star tells us its temperature. Red stars are coolest and blue stars are hottest.

Blue	White	Yellow	Orange	Red
45,000°F	18,000°F	10,800°F	8,500°F	6,000°F

28

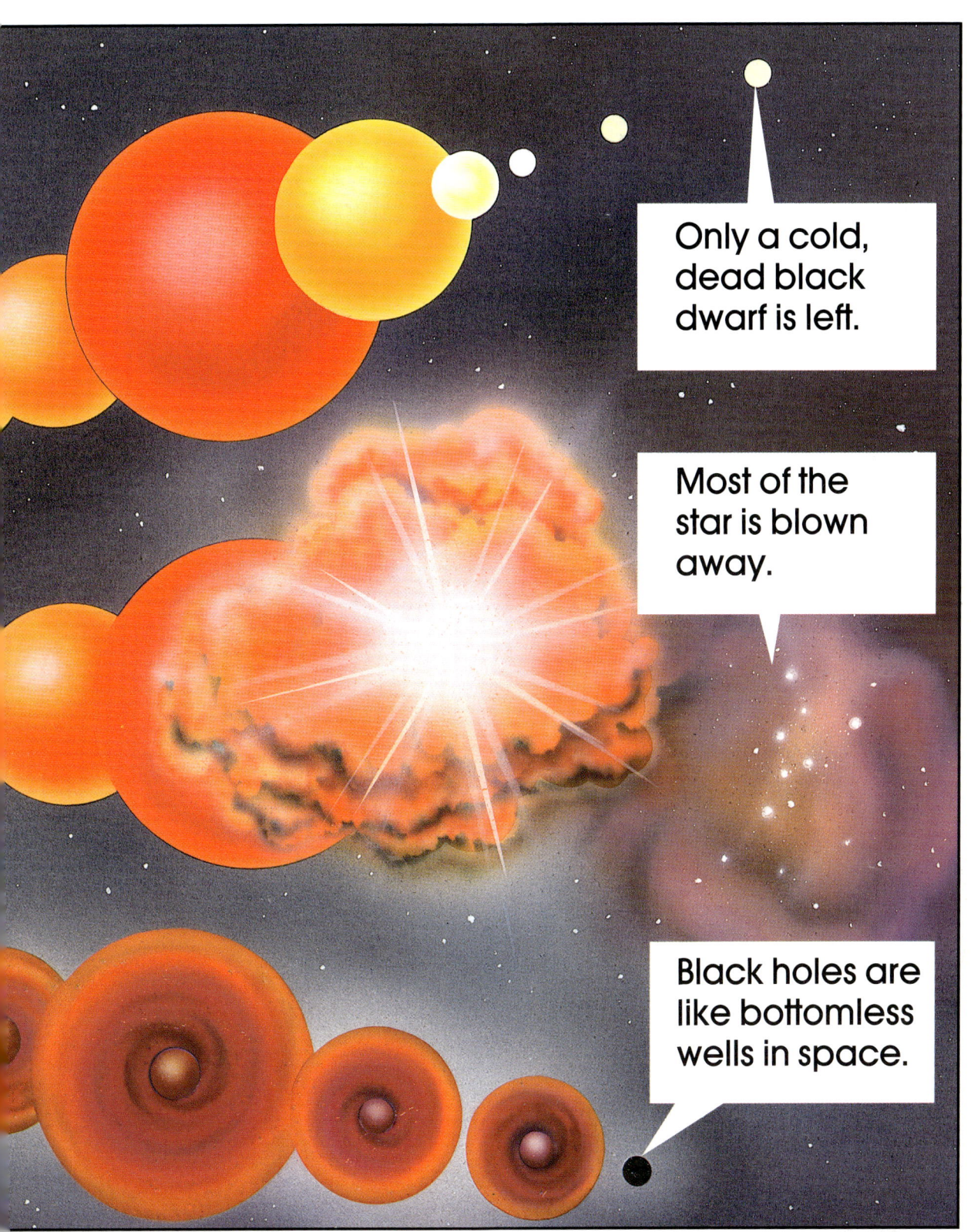

SOLAR POWER FACTS

This map shows how the Sun's rays fall on the Earth. The Earth gets more energy from the Sun than from all other fuels put together.

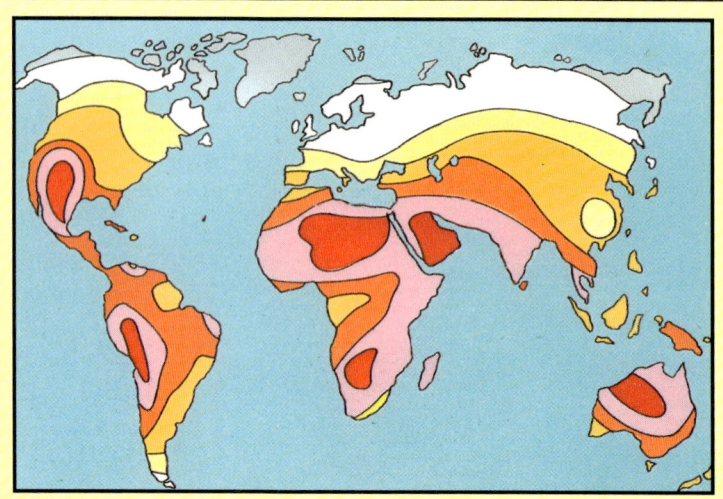

Red areas get most sunshine, white areas get least sunshine

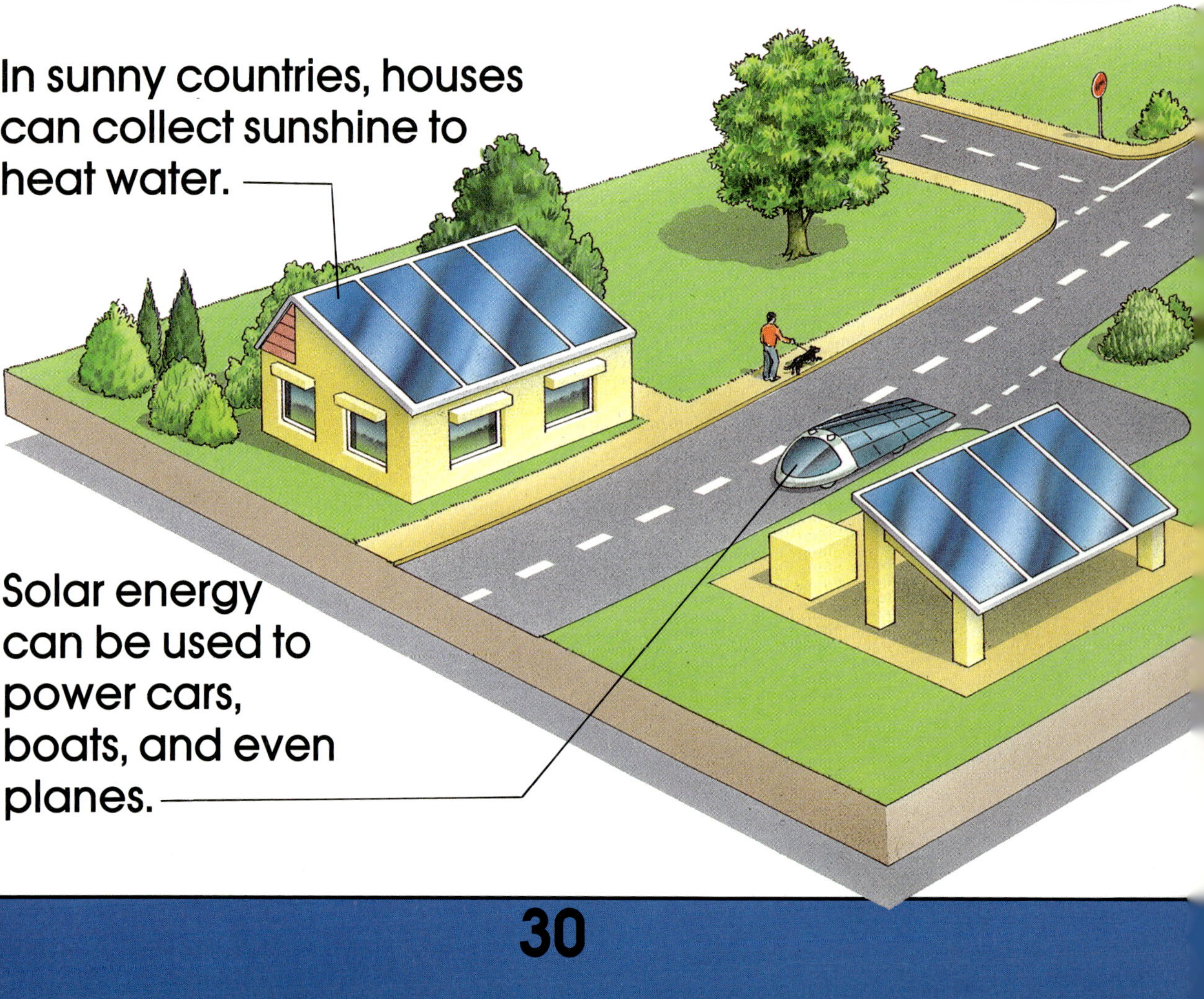

In sunny countries, houses can collect sunshine to heat water.

Solar energy can be used to power cars, boats, and even planes.

Even a calculator can be powered by the light from the Sun.

In future, satellites may be able to collect solar energy and beam it down to Earth.

Solar power plants use mirrors to collect sunshine. They use it to make electricity.

Solar power works well in space. There are no clouds to block the Sun's rays. A satellite's solar panels turn sunlight into electricity.

GLOSSARY

Gravity The force that pulls objects toward each other.

Light year The distance light travels in one year. This is about 5.8 trillion miles.

Planet A ball of substances which orbits the Sun. Planets are cold bodies which shine by reflecting light from the Sun.

Solar cells Units containing chemicals which turn sunlight into electricity.

Spectrum The name for the rainbow band of colors which makes up white light.

Star A huge ball of hot gas which shines because it makes energy at its core.

Universe All of space; everything that exists.

Index

birth of Sun 6
Black Holes 20, 21, 29

day and night 27
death of the Sun 22, 23

eclipses 18, 19

galaxies 20

heat 11, 16, 17

inside the sun 10

light 10, 14, 15
looking at the Sun 24, 25

photosphere 10
planets 8, 9

prominences 12, 13

solar energy 16, 17, 30, 31
Solar System 8, 9
stars 7, 20, 21 23, 28, 29
sunspots 12, 13

PHOTOCREDITS
Pages 5, 8 left and 31 bottom: Frank Spooner Pictures; pages 7, 12, 15, 17, 19 and 23: Spectrum Colour Library; page 8 right: David A. Hardy, FBIS, FISTC, LRPS; pages 13 and 20: Science Photo Library; page 16: The J. Allan Cash Photo Library; page 31 top: Roger Vlitos.